Trust Me, I've Tried

poetry written by
Varsha Iyer

Dedicated To

Evan Thomas Cummings

I am forever thankful to have stalked the #poetsofinstagram tag on social media two years ago and found your incredible work. I am forever thankful we decided to send each other our works in midst of writing books. I am forever thankful to have found a close friend, a confidante, an editor, a motivator, and everything in between.

To cultivate a super intimate relationship only through writing is something you don't see often and yet, here we find ourselves knowing each other's deepest darkest secrets because of words sent at 2AM. That kind of trust is one I have never experienced before but every day I am so happy we have cultivated it into a friendship so special.

I am endlessly inspired by you and your strength everyday that I have known you. I am so proud of everything you have accomplished, and I cannot wait to accomplish more together, side by side, bragging to everyone about our worn out books on our bookshelves and going on book tours cross country.

I am extremely grateful that you are always at the forefront of my messy emotions, digging to find the gold. And writing aside, I especially cannot thank you enough for being a damn good emotional support system when I don't even realize I need one— your words heal, help me grow.

Without you, not only would this book have never made it into a tangible, readible form— I would not be who I am today. You have eradicated my doubt a countless number of times and pushed me to be the absolute best writer I can be and I can only hope I return the favor. I am forever indebted to you.

Thank you for being my favorite writer, my favorite editor who edits their own dedication, and the best friend I could ask for. Next up— your book!

Preface

We are always searching for something, never quite fully at rest. The search is what keeps us motivated to keep moving, keep going— but what if I told you, there is no answer to your search? What you seek is constantly evolving and changing into different results? Each action, consequence yields a switch in what you thought you were searching for. If it all, how does that change your conquest? Would you learn how to fall in love with slowing down?

This complex pursuit of knowing the answers has always been something I've struggled with. This book, especially, as been an incredibly long, drawn-out process emotional process. I truly found it hard to finish it in its entirety—the content that sits heavily between these pages has been something I want to let go, have been trying to let go, and feel I am beyond ready to let go. For so long, my heart has felt stuck sifting through each word again and again. In all honesty, I feel it standing between me and growth. Thus began this incessant need to make sure this pain will be worth it— I really just want to make all this emotion bubbling inside of me worth it.

I asked myself multiple times what my purpose was in releasing this book. Though I'm still learning how to fall in love with slowing down, I realized with my writing, the purpose has always been to cultivate vulnerability at an uncertain age.

These emotions that have sat inside of me for the past year have been a strong, driving force in my growth— these experiences, these situations, these moments...without them, I would not be able to realize how quick life changes, how quick the questions I have for myself evolve into something else and then something other than that— this constant chase is imperative to who I am and how I can cultivate that vulnerability into something larger than what it started out to be, something better, something more impactful.

I am the people who make me who I am. I am the people who build me, invest in me, support me, love me, protect me, care for me. I am the people who taught me things in the past and the people who have yet to teach me things in the future— I cannot be sure of anything other than the fact that I am eager to learn and to keep learning.

This book is an accumulation of hard emotional work, unwounding of tightly wounded patterns, the depth of my heart wrapped in words in hopes that I can make you feel something real, something vulnerable. This one means more to me than the others and this one is both a beginning and an end to this written chapter of my life.

I ask you of only one thing as you read: please make a safe home for my words— nurture them, give them love and time to make their way into your thoughts and let it build roots inside of you. Let it change you as it has me.

Maybe we can create something beautiful with it, together.

there are times i stand in the shower: in moments
          of grief and in moments
          of sorrow
for a prolonged amount of time, until hot water
is not hot anymore, and i want it hotter—

i face backwards; water hitting my back
and my eyes fixated on the sunlight beam
coming from the window to the left of my shower.

          i try to grab it everytime, wishing i could
just take it in the palm of my hands and stuff it into a jar
and keep it— something so calm, so still

about the sunlight beam, it makes me cry.
i stare at the particles swimming in the light,
wondering how many have been swimming for so long
moving constantly— the sunlight beam is so still,
yet the dust cannot seem to stop moving.

i've never understood how to process grief;
it takes me time to deconstruct every particle
until finally, when i have turned the water off—

              —sunlight beams

what's your favorite part about yourself? i want to fall in love with it.
we believe in beauty because it's easy / we believe in beauty because we see it
in front of us. when we reach out into the future, when we look to the side
we see each other. the slight crease that forms in the corner of your eyes—
i'm in love with it, because your smile is born there. my eyes follow
down across your face to your lips that slant upward— my eyes start to brim with desire;
i've wanted something like this for so long, but i never understood it
and now it's in front of me and it's all i can understand. how—
does something trivial like a slight smile flip my world upside down
and tell me everything i've ever wanted to know, and *how*—
do i understand it so well?

what's your favorite flaw about yourself? i want to fall in love with it.
we believe in beauty because we know it's hard to come by / those moments
that catch our eyes as we pass by
but we stop to make that moment last forever;
we make time stop for us, and how— i love how you do that, baby, i love and i want
to make time stop for those moments, for me. we believe in beauty because
it's just like this— flaws and all, flaws and mistakes, flaws and improvements,
flaws and what i'm in love with. one by one, from where the feeling begins
at the bottom of your heart, and then on an upward path
until it finds another path and then another one— like a maze
yet we have the entirety of time to find the end /
and we've only just begun. and *how*—
do we understand it so well?

—mazes become simple when my lips touch yours

a singular look in a room full of people acts as a catalyst, and i
suddenly do not understand. a relatively simple concept
flips gravity the other way around, and suddenly, i am not pulled down.
only pulled up, towards something i cannot comprehend.
a catalytic beginning, and i'm trying to be analytical yet
this is something that cannot be pulled apart—

a singular moment, a singular look acts as a catalyst
to an emotion i didn't understand; a delayed reaction / weeks after
until your fingers traced the bare skin on my shoulder;
your lips on mine— easy, easy, easy, easy.

can you fall in love and then realize it later?
a relatively simple concept flips gravity the other way down;
and suddenly this becomes an anomaly— you are my anomaly.
how do you fall while being pulled up simultaneously?

i tend to ask questions to things that cannot be analyzed
so easily, and i push when i cannot, so easily, and i always move
towards something i cannot comprehend. the depth
of this anomaly refuses to be pulled apart and only pulled up
and my arms try to hold on and push up—
easy, easy, easy, easy and i laugh. a singular moment, a singular look
an anomaly— *you*— changed everything.

          —*will you be on the other side after i'm pulled up?*

have you ever seen something so beautiful you stop
in the midst of motion, and you take it in—
in the moment, you slow down, you halt,
you cannot take your eyes off of such beauty;

have you even closed your eyes and imagined being under a waterfall—
in the moment, you forget about everything else; it's just you
and the sound of rushing water so loud you cannot focus
on anything else, but— in the moment, you feel free.

have you ever seen something so idiosyncratic
you hesitate because you're unsure if it's real—
in the moment, you slow down, you take time
to deconstruct until you've constructed a complete thought;

have you even struggled to find words for something
you don't know where to begin to search—
in the moment, you remember every past definition of beauty and fail
to see the similarity because this is different—

in the moment, this feels new.

have you ever seen something so incredible
your heart skips beats on an alternate rhythm—
in the moment, you speed up, you frantically desire,
you want what you've dipped your toes into;

have you ever wanted to sink your whole body under water—
in the moment you're submerged into a cascading waterfall
until you cannot hear anything anymore
and it's a silent solace and if you focus you can hear—

in the moment, it's just you and i

—and i drown into you

spent so long, trying
to find a rhythm i once had—
not realizing, that song has been over
ten songs ago. i tried
and i tried to find the tune
i had forgotten in an attempt
to feel okay—
not realizing the beat has changed
and the orchestra has been playing different chords,
softer and slower—
much more calmly than before,
to make me realize,
this is a new song.

—new rhythms

my favorite color wasn't green until i met you.
imagine a room filled with plants, you in the middle, and me—
maybe on some level i already knew, like you—
i was just too far away from it / to see clearly,
i have to step forward and to step forward,
i have to let go of what i was holding onto. and so i did—
they call that blind faith. i call it seeing green.

my favorite color wasn't green until i met you.
it was black— a void of color, a void of obscured truths.
nothing made sense and i assumed that was normal.
oh, how i should've known never to settle for the ordinary
when the extraordinary exists within you.

my favorite color wasn't green until i met you.
and then you wrote, "you're my favorite hue of green,"
and i fell in love with that line. i looked up every hue of green—
searching for one that reminded me of you.
suddenly, hues of green weren't enough— i wanted you.

my favorite color wasn't green until i met you.
imagine a room filled with plants, you in the middle, and me—
all i see is green— shades of it— and then you—
i see trees so tall and leaves so bright and stems so strong,
you and i in seas of greens, waves crashing wildly,
floating beside one another in our favorite hues.

                    —*light olive looks good with dark forest green, don't you think?*

life won't let me grieve. i've asked nicely—
i've asked patiently, but i never get an answer back.
everytime there is silence, it is immediately replaced
for silence is filled with reality and the reality of it is that i am unable to grieve.
i've asked, and i've asked, and i've contemplated the if's and whys and buts—
and yet, the silence is deafening; the white noise grows in my head
so i raise the volume of the same song i've had on repeat
for the past six hours— i cannot stop thinking about the next thing i have to do;
leaping into the future before the present is completed.

life still works— like a machine fighting through its kinks
and its broken parts, the wheels rotate faster and with more fervor
as if the damage only drives determination;
and grief can only be fought with failing to grieve.

we wage war with what we can handle but when we face grief,
the only thing that can be conquered is pain. instead, we wage
war with the silence and pretend our enemies do not exist.

is that what we do?
we move, despite—
we continue, despite—
we act, despite—
i am tired of *despite*.

i cannot think about the silence without feeling sick;
the reality of it all is that i am unable to grieve.

i've asked nicely— i've asked patiently. with more damage done,
i run faster— moving at a continuous pace unaware of where i'm going,
unknowingly towards the silence that grows larger by the day.
the song that is stuck on repeat sounds so good,
and i would hate for it to stop suddenly— despite;

silence is already filled with reality and the reality is that—
i cannot escape from what i know it true: grief is inevitable.

—but the song has been over for hours and now i face the silence

16

Varsha Iyer

when angels sleep, i awake. i've always felt a little off center
        my wings are always matted, knotted, so i use scissors i find
in my mother's closet, and i cut—

i am overwhelmed with memories of a little girl— me,
hiding in between sweaters hanging above my head and
pants folded beneath; i am hidden in the nook
of the scent of jasmine and my mother's lips on my cheek
as she tells me she's so proud of me—

the way i cut is not even, and it looks crooked like the shape of my nose
and i want to cry— i've never liked comments about my face
and hearing, "*you're pretty*," sits uneasy in my gut so i throw up.

when angels sleep, i stare at their wings. white, unmangled, clean—
        soft is the only similar thing between me and them;
my mother's lips feel like a nice home for me, i want to go hide back in them
        until i feel secure, while my uneven cuts become even;

growth is messy, and i am too

              —the angel who never slept

and for every 11:11, i make a wish— to make forever,
last longer than forever can be, with you.
your secrets are safe with me, and i— with you,
tell me, baby, if i tell you every wish i make—
will you keep them safe in the palm of your hands?

technically, a wish is intangible, yet
with you, they're real. tell me, baby, how every 11:11
wish i have made since i've met you has come true?
from the beginning— until longer than forever can be,
i have never felt so free, staring up at the sky
and then at you— just something about it, huh?

i want to grab each star i see, regardless of whether they burn or not
and give them to you. i want to give you the universe—
i want to make the intangible, tangible for you.

and for every 11:11, i make a wish— to freeze time
so forever can last longer than forever can be,
because forever with you is not long enough—
tell me, baby, if i give you my heart—
will you keep it safe in the palm of your hands?

theoretically, a wish is intangible. and yet,
with you, they're real. the math is easy to do:
my heart with you is the safest place it could be—
and how many wishes do i have to make
so you'll have it forever
longer than forever can be?

—(my heart + you) x wishes i have to make

Varsha Iyer

i've never met a man
who matched my eloquence—
until i met you
we write in circles, we talk in circles
we learn on a line that's sloped upwards—

there is always so much more to understand
and to listen to each other so intently
with ears tilted slightly and lips pursed in concentration, in genuine desire
your lips teach me something new everyday

i have never felt more thankful for eloquence in its entirety—
something so simple always contains layers
of knowledge, and of wonder
teach me everything and i'll teach you what i can

until i met you, i wrote but i never really understood
i would talk, but i never really listened
i've never met a man who matched my eloquence—

—until i met you

i want to pull you close— by the silver around your neck,
imagine you in silver and me in gold—side by side,
like a king and a queen on a marble throne that the king has built;
with his strong hands, he holds me so well— and it makes me smile,
endlessly until it's stuck there.

i want to pull you close by the silver on your neck.
when i close my eyes i see things more clearly—
baby, you're the piece of peace of mind i've been needing
and the answer to a question i've been asking for far too long—
can clarity exist when nothing is clear at all?

you've never seen a queen kneel by her king— yet,
here i am. side by side, gold by silver, obscurity by clarity and yet,
and yet, i've said yet four times. twice more,

not knowing what comes next and yet, ready
for what i know comes next in the same line of vision. and yet,
i want to pull you so so close— by the silver on your neck,
imagine you in silver and me in gold—side by side,
until there is no more space in between and only above.

you've never seen a queen kneel for her king— yet,
here i am. side by side, gold by silver, obscurity by clarity and yet,
and yet, i've said yet four more.

—424

20

Varsha Iyer

i've witnessed the many lives of your lips. from the beginning, i've been drawn
towards the shapes they take and i can't help but move closer. they say such sweet things,
did you know? lips are a hundred times more sensitive than your fingertips, and i
would love to heighten the feeling until all you can feel is my lips on yours.

the many lives of your lips carry the weight of a hundred wise men.
from the beginning, i've watched and i've memorized each curve when you concentrate,
each slanted line when you smile, and when you wonder, your upper lip take the shape
of the silhouette of two hills side by side and your bottom lips draws me in, baby
i want to know what you wonder— until i'm wondering too,
from the beginning, i've been drawn to the longing of wanting your lips
to feel what mine feel for you.

they say such sweet things, and the many lives of your lips make me swell
with overwhelming waves of love, crashing against mine— baby i want to know
each life and each shape and each curve and each line
until the feeling is so heightened all you can feel is my lips on yours.
my lips have been slanted in awe since they met yours. i'm so drawn
to the many lives of your lips and i vow to live in each one
until i've memorized whatever can be
until i've made home in the crashing waves.

—the many lives of your lips

the day i met anger, i fell to my knees
my arms were outstretched in front of me
my heart detached itself from my body
and i vomited it directly into my palm

it felt so good to let go
of the thing that had deeply rooted itself into me

it felt so good to let go

the aftertaste of my heart was almost sweet,
a craving— i sometimes feel it now

the day i met anger, i never felt so understood
something so questionable; its intentions
and its reactions and its actions and its consequences
and its being was so certain, so induspitable

i let go, in order to feel alone
with the one emotion people fight to avoid feeling

the day i met anger, i fell in love
there is a method to how we break ourselves down,
and there is a method to how we ended up angry in the first place

the aftertaste of anger is almost too sweet,
a craving— i feel it more often than i ever would've imagined

to be understood is a risky game,
and to be understood by anger is even riskier—
but here i am, palms outstretched, ready to give it everything

—the day i met anger, i asked it to take my heart and make sense of it for me

Varsha Iyer

i would eat the stars that fill the morning sky just to impress you;
i would grow lemon trees at the base of my stomach;
the finest wines cannot compete with the grapes my eyes will cry out for you—

the roots that sprout from my spine grow to kiss your forehead; so sweet,
water it, will you? feed it, let it wrap around you just as it has me;
oh, *sweetheart* these lemons taste so good, they pair well with the wine
that pours out of my eyes; eat them whole

—and i will eat the stars that fill the morning sky

let's put our egos aside for just one moment. let's
take this wrong moment— dismantle it for all it is worth
and maybe, we could find millions of right moments inside.

that's the funny thing about ego. the heaviness is not
what clouds us from moving forward but obstructs us
from understanding what is / what can / what will be real.

for one moment, let's. take this wrong moment and see through it,
like a glass that fragments all the right moments for us; we understand, ego aside—
there is just too much right in wrongs to feel wrong about the rights we find.

—let's

Varsha Iyer

he's curious because he cares, he's concerned
and i love when.
he asks,
something new each sunrise
and ends with the same question, in whispers, at sunset.

well-versed in thought,
well-versed in my thought,
he's curiously careful; curious, as to, me— careful, with my fragility

he's concerned, and i love when.
he is so sweet to me,
he asks,
how we can be well-versed together,
and if two thoughts can co-exist at the same time; such as:

i love you, and i love your thoughts.

at high intensities, we think. we ask,
well-versed in how we tell each other we love the other,
well-versed in thought, my thought.
careful, and curious— and i love when.

—he asks, "are you my baby?"

we've driven many miles— and i've been counting.
for these thoughts that accumulate in my head
to form the words my mouth has been wanting to say.
it's harder than i thought—
how, how, *how* does one man make me so weak in the knees—
and how, how, *how* does it not matter how much i run,
how much i sweat, cry, laugh, try to make myself stronger?
none of it matters, and i end up counting. i drive many miles
to get to you, to make sense of it all;
and yet, my knees still give out in front of me, i see your words
and i see you. i see you, and you, make it make sense. it's all i want to see.
for these thoughts that accumulate in my head are the same thoughts
you whisper to me late at night and i whisper back—
counting the sweet things you say seems arbitrary
because i know i'll be counting until my last breath, so i keep driving;
i keep inhaling,
exhaling;
i keep my foot on the gas—
these miles rack up, but still they're endless.
i haven't run out of gas in months; i never stop to park.
i see you, and *you*, make it make sense.

—i stopped counting at around 1,000 miles

Varsha Iyer

waves know shores, and i know you— it hasn't been much time
yet it's been years / seconds slow down, and time proves to not be real.

sands know hermit crabs and seashells, and i burrow deep beneath the ground
to conserve warmth. i rest my head in the crook of your neck— it's the simple details
of how algae floats along with the sea, of how we rock back and forth
until high tides lull into slow ones— and our breaths mimic each other.

waves know shores, and i know you— it hasn't been much time
yet it's been years / and the moon has gone through so many phases,
and my heart tries to mimic the beats of yours; they float together as they should.
and i stay— my body so close to yours. curved like crescents slowly shifting, waning

and it's the simple details— to conserve warmth, it feels wrong to move my body
away from yours. to create the illusion of ripples, i'll bring my lips to yours
waiting, until the moon waxes into a full moon and the cycle repeats again.

—many moons, many nights, many tides

i hope my words find their way to you, no matter how far away you stand.
still, i keep writing because writing never seems to satiate what i feel—

the more i deconstruct, the more i'm told some things are superficial
and only mean what they mean. digging more means you will find less
than what your mind has already started to assume.

form works— hand in hand— with function

and i straighten my back when i realize i have been slumped for hours, aching.
no matter how far away you stand, i hope my words find their way to you.

now, i cannot stop writing even after i have finished what i have wanted to say;
this need to satiate what i feel derives dangerous assumptions about the depth
i hold for myself and digging more means you will find more. it never ends— so

—make it mean something; if not, let it mean nothing

Varsha Iyer

tenderly, care for the me that exists in your mind —
i've been writing these songs that have no tunes in my sleep,
if we could rule the world, would you let me be your queen?

lately, that's all i've been thinking about —
i dream you have the instruments to make the music
i so badly wished my words had; mythopoeic

stories that manifests us as a king and queen;
tenderly, care for the me that exists in your mind —

i've been writing these songs that have no tunes
in hopes i'll find my way back home to you.

— my favorite songs are the ones i haven't heard yet

the role you are attempting to play does not exist.
so create it from scratch. what do you have to lose?

the roles we play get messy / you and i switch parts—
parts of you, parts of me / we forget where we began so we just continue.

for every wrong answer, there is a right question.

the role you are attempting to play does not exist.
so create it from scratch. what do you have to lose?

the roles we play get messy / you and i play the same part—
is the glass half empty or half full? baby, you tell me.

for every wrong answer, there is a right question.

—what do you have to lose?

Varsha Iyer

you fit into me, like a new moon
in the night sky; look to it— *there*, do you see
the outline of a curve? does it remind you of how
your hand curves into my right hypochondriac region?
you fit into me, and i tell you: we can share the stars
in the night sky; *look*, point to the ones that are yours—
i'll take them in my hand and eat them; i will be just as bright
and we can climb a ladder into the sky. you fit into me,
like exceedingly rare astronomical moments. as if we are
Universes side by side. from here, we can see how the earth
spins so quick, if i could tell it to slow down—for a moment,
until your hand melts into my ribs; the heat of unidentified
Suns casts shadows we sleep in before we wake. we look,
we stay / *easily* / we watch / we fit / into / space.

                    —*we are / we are Spiral NGC 4414's*

31

my sweetheart, lean back— i have built a planetarium for you. close your eyes
for a second and imagine. as we move, everything moves with us;
yet, we don't slow down. maybe that's why i keep falling for you a bit more every night.

we watch together, we lean back— the way celestial bodies form in front of our eyes isn't
in the least bit magical; it's the speed in which it happens / it happens as we kiss under
these stars that blink once, twice / when we move, everything moves with us.

my sweetheart, i fall for you harder every night and i have built a planetarium for you.
lean back so we can count the galactic formations on our fingers until we run out,
counting how many "i love you's," we can fit in one galaxy until the next one forms.
we never slow down, my sweetheart; i will build as many planetariums as you want.

—count the stars with me

Varsha Iyer

the clouds stand still
for those whose thoughts
are the sole architect of their actions.

these thoughts, they never cease
and i like to watch.

i watch the cloudless skies,
i watch the birds make flight from tree to tree,
i watch the breeze make itself visible through leaves
that are so, so green. i think of you

i think of us, the clouds stand still
for those whose thoughts
are endless, i like to watch them go by.

            —the sky is cloudless but i see clouds

i've had intimate conversations with my plant about you. last week
i watched as the brightest leaf on my pothos started curling; i watched and i cried.
it was the first plant i have ever cared for— you gave it to me.
the first night, we wept together.
my heart felt heavier than usual, my eyes even more so.
my mouth felt dry, yet i spoke:
"are you scared?"—
i thought about how it probably had no idea what was happening to its limb,
an extension of itself slowly folding into itself,
an extension of my sadness seeping into it.
i thought about how the brightest leaf turned dark within a sunset.

i've had intimate conversations with my plant about you. last week
you said *"i love you,"* for the first time and funny,
i had been wanting to say it the week prior.
when i got home, i watered my pothos, still curled; i watched and i cried.
the second night, i prayed.
i never really believed in God, i vowed that religion was too complicated
to deconstruct, to pull apart right now— i simply didn't have the time,
and yet it felt right to pray to my plant.
falling to my knees, head to my chin, eyes closed:
"ease my fears,"—
my fingers are reached out gently touching a leaf,
softness comes with a price, softness comes when you least expect it.

can peace coexist with obscurity; can clarity be undisturbed in such turbulent waters?

i've had intimate conversations with my plant about you. last week
i watered my pothos, again and the next day, i watched.
and again. the cycle continues
until curled leaves unfurl, and intimate conversations start to become more common,
with each leaf, with each stem, with each grain of soil,
until peace starts to float among rushed waves.

—intimate conversations

Varsha Iyer

thy words seem to find home in mine pulse, intuitively—
billow me under; listen close— from thy fingertips they dawn

i ask of depth, and receive verily, apace with no deliberation
soft touches turns to salacious moments, and mine lips tend to inquire

of false-heart: art we worthy of being desired? am i— i ponder:
if our virtues claim to be seminal to who we art; am i redeeming of thy heart?

such desolate asks need not be questioned for thy vows; full of ardor
beget a notion that cannot be matched— *but of course! ad infinitum*—

thine kisses graze like a summer's breeze in improbable heat; implicit words
thou hast yet to write— mine worries cease; thy effortless penmanship billows me under

science of love is not imperative to those who art already in love;
thy words seem to find a home in mine pulse— skipping, leaping into mine bloodstream;

the vast oceans and seas art unfortunate for they cannot conceive
thy love penned in ink; for they art not merely enough,
hath the tides been stronger; we could have lived among waters

flowing to our own accord; wilt thou ardor keep with
turbulence amongst the current? effectuate the tides to align with my pulse—
soft touches turn to salacious moments; lingering for good reason, such good reason.

thy locutions soak into me, implicit and scripted; i often hear it lost at sea—
i believe: bid me to be thine, and i am thine; sung like a summer's breeze,
i could say it— *ad infinitum*!

i would want to kiss thy written words a thousand times.
be my poetry; be each verse, be— if all it takes is pen to paper, intimately—
be til thy words nestle deep in me; worries wilting into breezes

that touch upon mine lips; i think of thee— thy letters penned in ink— *i am home*—
art we in love? art we worthy of feeling this way? art we— we art, we art—
at sea, in summer's breeze, in archaic poetry.

—billow me under for i am wholly yours

the slight difference between romance and love— we fit in between,
we make simple moments expand into something sublime,
we make romance seem much more than love, and vice versa.

there are moments i feel almost giddy, my heart moves
rapidly in between romance and love, trying to find a position
of peace / i laugh a lot / at peace / i cannot stop smiling.

the slight difference between romance and love— it's a gap
that we've explored; every inch has been scoured, every definition redefined,
every moment turned into a longer one yet time still proves to be endless.

new worlds appear at our fingertips, and i want to let you name them.
they are larger than the ones we've lived in prior. they are filled
of peace / my heart flips / at peace / i cannot stop falling for you.

—giddy / at peace

"well, we have to have a lemon tree in our backyard."
"of course, darling."
"but— how does it work? how long does it take for a lemon tree to grow?"
"three years, for it to reach its full maturity, for it to start growing lemons."
"what if we get one that's two years old, and then watch it grow for its last year?"
"no, baby, if we get a lemon tree— we have to watch its growth from the beginning,"
his sweet voice sounds like a summer's tune in my ear. mesmerizing as i daydream,
"we," i say.
"*we*," he replies.

—*a lemon tree, and we makes three*

the first person my mind runs to when i see something beautiful is you
like a perpetual yearning, i have your heart on my mind
it's sitting comfortable, safe—
i'd give you kisses with my fingertips while your eyes close in comfort—
isn't that all love is?

when a leaf starts wilting and slightly browning, we shift
we move towards the light and yet, we cannot always live in the light
we perpetually yearn for a greater meaning
we look towards the root of plants, we repot, we water
when i see something beautiful, my mind only wants to run to you

isn't that all love is?
it both illuminates and unmoors when the moon is turning away
we shift like glasses of water that are half full and half empty
because we have given it to the plant in front of us
we look at the greener leaves and find comfort—

you are made up of things i cannot explain
and my mind is held only by your heart

when your eyes close, the dreams that you don't dream seep into me
when i see something beautiful, i dream of you
precariously holding onto each kiss i give you, you walk into the sun
we sometimes forget if the light is too intensely bright, all you see is dark
when you wake, i will have a glass of water, half full and half empty
because i had the same nightmare as you
i'll stay by your side until we fall sleep again

isn't that all love is?
a perpetual yearning to see beauty in both darkness and light
and leaves that wilt and leaves that start to brown and leaves that are so green
i have your heart wrapped in my head— safe
slow and steady— we shift

you are made up of things i cannot explain
and that is the most beautiful thing i have seen in a very long time

—isn't that?

Varsha Iyer

i've been feeling a little fragile lately— my edges sharp enough to make you bleed.
tell me how you can say all the right things but i still need more— an insatiable need
to want to curve my edges; i hate to watch you bleed. i can taste the rust on my tongue
and i want to dig my fingers deep into myself— breaking it apart, each fragile piece
and each fragile edge ready to be curved and hand it to you.

—in an attempt to help you help me

you ask me what depth means, and now— i finally understand.
                    you are deeply flawed. i see it;
i am afraid i have crawled into each flaw, smothering myself
into what i have already known for weeks— your depth
is what prevents you from seeing clearly. we have to fight
harder to crawl out of the depths of ourselves— i see it;
my depth and your depth tangled in knots; i am in love
with all of your flaws, despite— i finally understand.
                to see clearly, you ask me what depth means.

          —how do i make you understand?

minuet is a dance. form meeting function

it should be cohesive, concise, fluid
it should not follow

hand in hand, eye to eye

the intention— a marriage between logic and insanity
hand in hand, eye to eye

and the duality within life
forms and its functionality.
      metaphors and reality coming together
      very writer-esque
      yes
      the philosophy within it all!

each step is necessary
its the wireframe of like a black hole and white hole singularity

its practically a wormhole
but a seemingly perpetual loop
every exit is a new idea

          —a text conversation between you and i
          back in april about starting functional design studio

it's all in the subtleties—
we drive on I-85 late at night
the windows are half way down in January
and i have never felt so warm before
we listen to Sadé's greatest hits on repeat
i kiss your cheek in between songs
you tell me that you are in love with me
and that i am making you feel again
i tell you that you are deeper than divine
and you are all that i think about
and that i am falling with blind faith

it's all in the subtleties—
how did we end up at a 5-star restaurant in sweats?
and how are we the only two people in this crowded place?
you ask, "do you think they look at us and see how in love we are?
two lovers just so encapsulated with each other—"
that night, i understood what love really meant
love isn't love anymore, love is *you*

it's all in the subtleties—
in the middle of a furniture store
we sit in all the chairs, we look at dining tables
we dream of our home
covered in mid-century modern chairs
the walls painted in our shades of green and our shades of cream
we take pictures though we won't forget
my heart often flips at the sight of you
that night, it leapt into your hands
and made a home there

it's all in the subtleties—
we lay in bed together, arms tightly wrapped
my head nestled in the crook of your neck
lips pressed up against every inch of you i can find
whispering sweet words written about each other
we pine, we ache, we leap
eating vegan banana bread hungrily
laughing, watching movies that make us cry
feeling you, loving you—
kissing again and again and again because once, twice is never enough
feeling so much as moments multiply and expand
as moments turn into forevers; another forever with you

—forevers, forever with you

everywhere you look, there are circular mirrors. we reflect
what we think / we understand what we want / we see
each other, hand in hand / everywhere you look.
there are circular mirrors, and we covet the future
precariously. i want to create,
hand me downs,
with you. building circular mirrors as large as we can make them.
we reflect what we think / we see each other, hand in hand /
everywhere you look, everything comes full circle
i hand you another mirror
to covet, to understand

     —our future

when you say, "i know, i know," and pull me close,
        my heart aches. for you, i will
never give up. please, i know, i know what you whisper in the dark so sweet, so lovingly
and i miss it every time i close my eyes. i imagine when you say in that sweet, loving way
"i know, i know," you think of me, oh how i love to be held by you,
        my heart aches. for you, i will
let you keep all of my love. i don't want any of it anymore, it belongs with you
and i ask, *please*, never give up. when you say, "i know, i know," and pull me close
        to kiss my forehead. again and again and again so sweet, so lovingly
and to hold me tight, until i've given you all that i have, again and again and again
        my heart aches. for you, i will
imagine being pulled so close, your lips at my ear, telling me, "you know. you know,"

        —i love that you always know, you just know

let's sit in silence for two hours. we can
do anything but speak; for two hours let's
enjoy the sensation as it builds inside of us.

how many days have passed before you sat up
thinking: "*something needs to change*." how
many thoughts have you thought out thoroughly?

let's sit in silence for two hours. my hands will
tell yours stories— my lips will touch the temples
of your head, tenderly; for two hours let's just be.

                                   —silent stories have more weight

"there is a difference between: being alone, and *being* alone."
i act like i understand but i don't.
if i'm being honest, i never understood.
i want to ask: "why do you hate it so much?"
i write it down on paper as if ink will make it easier for me to see the difference.
but ink won't sharpen lines that are blurred,
and things that are smeared cannot be made clear.
"there is a difference between: you and me."
i act like i understand but i don't.
if i'm being honest, we are more alike than we are not.
empathy and apathy are born from the same mother—
she bares so much burden;
she gave all of her worries to her first born— empathy,
and gave all of her love to her second child— apathy.
when they meet, they mourn their mother who seems to make a home in alienation.
i find myself alone with my thoughts— frequently, fervently
i like being alone, i like *being* alone.
i want to ask: "why do you hate it so much?"
i act like i understand, so i don't.
i sink thick into blurred lines and smeared feelings
and i let myself weep.
if i'm being honest, maybe there is a difference between you and me.
if i'm being honest, you've never wept for me. if i'm being honest,

—alienation makes things clear for me, and makes things too real for you

Varsha Iyer

how many seconds have passed
where my lips hath not touched thine,
love hath not been spoken by either;
how many seconds have passed
until we return home again?

—*watching the clock move*

i ate all the stars in the sky
and burned my mouth. now, i ache—
i should have known, right?

constellations cannot be digested; maybe
depending on their brightness; maybe
if i had been more careful; maybe—

i ate all the stars in the sky and now,
my eyes cannot stop seeing colors; they overwhelm
me into seeing nothing. i am full, but—

—i am empty

Varsha Iyer

i miss you. i miss you, i miss you, i miss you. i throw it up
on the side of the street, at the end of the night
i've refrained—
and now my throat is itchy and i want to pry my fingers down
my mouth so i can calm it down
oh, how it hurts to not be able to tell you
but i've refrained, and yet—
nothing changes.

—missing someone is prehaps more complicated than loving them

i've left traces of myself everywhere you step
in every mirror you look in, on your bookshelf—
what do you keep from me in your silence
what do you think about when you see the lock i gave you
locked tightly around your neck
what do you see when you look up at the sky
and remember planetariums make you feel
like you're the only one in space like you've always dreamed of
what do you design when you read about Frank Lloyd Wright
and see the house we dreamed of building
what do you say to yourself on top of mountains
when you hike, when you forget about the world and it's just you
when you tell me you're safe, you're safe, you're safe

i've had a recurring daydream lately, i see it everywhere i step
every mirror i look in, on my bookshelf—
i freeze oranges just to see how they would taste
i've been having trouble finding the right keys
for each lock i come across
i recreate the night sky on my ceiling with my projector
and i cry at the stars
i swim in oceans to show you
the depth of my heart
i close my eyes and float and it's just me
it's just me and it's okay
and i tell you i'm safe, i'm safe, i'm safe
even if i haven't been since you left

—what do you keep from me in your silence?

Varsha Iyer

the prettiest pictures of myself sit inside the roll of film you never got developed.
i've never felt so pretty, sitting inside something before— still,
i've never felt so pretty, posing against the wall of a parking deck, buzzed off
of frozen peach margaritas and your kisses. i licked off all the salt around my cup
and yours because i liked the way it tasted against your tequila flavored lips.
i've never felt so pretty, pushed up against that wall hearing your voice
tell me you wanted to fill your rolls of film with pictures of me— "what else
could possibly be better?" i've never felt so pretty, rolled up delicately
inside that roll of film— motionless / separated from reality / distant.

the prettiest pictures of myself sit inside the roll of film you never got developed.
i've never felt so pretty, slow dancing in middle of the park with you
to the live music echoing through cloudless skies buzzed off of frozen
peach margaritas, hearing your voice tell me you'd peel peaches for me
and make fresh peach juice and swallow slices of peaches until we were drunk.
i've never felt so pretty, watching you fall asleep on my lap with your hand
intertwined in mine— i've never felt so pretty, feeling your sweet and salty lips kiss
my thigh lazily mid-slumber. i've never felt so pretty knowing
you have a roll of film filled with how i look when i'm in love.

i've never felt so pretty knowing you have a roll of film filled with lips covered
in salt from peachy margaritas and peaches and cream chapstick from your lips and
smiles so wide and kisses so deep and futures forgotten. i've never felt so pretty,
rolled up delicately inside that roll of film— motionless / separated from reality / distant.

—i've never felt so pretty sitting inside undeveloped film

love is the one thing i cannot perform; and watching you
act makes me want to walk on a path that is billowed with trees.

how many leaves on trees can i see until i get tired? see,
there is no right or wrong answer but a right path of progression.

moving forward is the hardest thing you will have ever had to do
but the easiest thing to do in this specific, singular moment.

if i cannot make you believe that acting is always based on reality,
i cannot make you see the reality of it all— the leaves are so green

when i look at you, the leaves are so green / when i look into your eyes,
the leaves are so green / when i hear your voice, the leaves are so green

—and scene

your existence has grown to be so big inside of me—
there are so many voices in my head, i've almost forgotten
all of them until i'm reminded again. out of all, i miss yours
the most—intrinsic value is invaluable at this point;
seconds pass and they still feel like forevers. i say your name
again and again in my sleep until you show up. and i watch you
go so easily; swallowing my existence while walking over
the ground we used to lay on so often. i miss it the most—
counting the steps we take until we are tired but now i count
the steps i take until i vomit your existence. it takes the shape
of four kisses, then two, then four again. what a logical thing
to do— each forever broken down is invaluable at this point
in time and yet, i say your name again and again in my sleep
until you tell me: "*the past was the past. the future isn't real.
wake up. vomit until i am out of your system.*"

—waiting for the moment you're gone

do the birds say goodbye when they depart from each other,
traveling so close— together, traveling so far— and just like that,
they separate. do they say goodbye or do they sigh in relief
when their wings feel more free when the air is more empty
and the fresh wind hits their feathers so light— they've been waiting
for this moment, together, traveling so far— separately.

—maybe they're okay only to know they will reunite once again

Varsha Iyer

they say to love someone long-term is to attend a thousand funerals
of the person they used to be. i'm mourning now, grieving comes next—
rinse, repeat until i'm in love with someone new, in you. in this cyclical pattern,
i forget patterns are meant to be broken before they can be rebuilt.
i weep for the moment i started to fall in love with you, desperate to rewind time
and sit in that moment until i've memorized every detail—
if i had wings, i would fly over rivers and through canyons to see if you
had been peaceful throughout each life or if there was something you regretted—
my wings flutter at every funeral, each feather falling in hopes moments we shared
are immortalized and you remember all the rivers i've flown across to meet you again.

—when you see an old picture of us, do you miss me?

i hope you find a pulse in your loneliness,
the same one that rises when my lips touch yours.
i've locked the door, and yet i check three more times
and when i walk down the driveway,
i remember each time i would look at the sky before
you would pull up. i used to count the stars,
the things we want to change
are never things we can, i know, and yet
i try three more times. have you found a pulse yet?
each time i water my plants, i remember
you were with me for each i bought / you gave
when you didn't want. how could i be angry at that?
i used to count the stars, standing on my heels
almost tripping over my feet every time
but your headlights coming into view would bring me back
every time. back then, i would forget to lock my door.
and now, i check three times. the things we want to change
cannot be changed by force. so i let it go,
and look. these plants are growing so much /
i'm giving them everything they want. i hope
i stop using hope as a flaw, soon. i think i'm learning

—i can't count all the stars, except the beat of my own pulse

whenever you'd get in my car,
you would turn the volume off on my maps
because you would swear you would
tell me the way. i remember i used to
instinctively look— just in case, just to be
sure and you would always roll your eyes
and tell me to trust you.

the passenger seat of my car
has been left untouched after you got out
for the last time. i was so busy
trying to find the trust i left with you
i forgot to turn the voice in my phone
back on so i could leave this perfect,
pretty picture of where i envisioned
we would arrive.

the first few times i drove, i got lost.
i almost liked it that way— i found
bits and pieces of my trust flattened
on the road; road and street names
blurred themselves with silence.
sometimes i still instinctively look
at the passenger seat of my car,
just in case you're there to tell me
how to find my way back home.

—when i turned the voice on my maps back on,
for a second i hoped it would be yours

do not seek what you have not
been giving to yourself;
do not seek refuge

without understanding
what a refuge consists of.
pursue with no agenda, build—

a home built with your own hands
feels more secure when others help
build, rather than build it all for you.

do not seek what you have not
for what you are missing, is what
others will seek from you.

—pursue all persons with no agenda, only

Varsha Iyer

there's a lot of pain in my heart, and i've tried
to let it go. i have— but the deeper my nails dig into
my flesh in order to reach my heart, more of it
resurfaces. it's like a game of checkers— but,
we make up the rules because the rules never applied.
i've tried to let it go— but now, my heart is skipping
beats to get to somewhere i've never been; faster
until i've calmed it down— i have. my nails dig so deep
until my fingers are knuckle deep in blood; the red
matches the color of my eyes; i haven't slept in so long—
and i've tried; playing checkers is boring to me now;
i need a new game with new rules to catch up to my heart.
there's a lot of pain, and it won't let up— it won't end;
so it comes up and up and up; i've got a better way to play
when the rules don't exist. so i let my fingers twist and i let
my nails stain red until they've let go of what resurfaces.

                    —*until then, clear the board. flip it. break it in two.*

if there's nothing you hold sacred, what will you stand for?
there's anger in my skin that creates an itch in my throat.
it always hurts around 3AM when i usually would hang up
the phone because you had fallen asleep. now, i wake up
and drink two full glasses of ice cold water and stay up to watch
the sunrise. how quiet the world is when no one is awake,
how quiet it is to feel like the only one alive. what will you stand for,
if what you held sacred now cannot stand you? you ask me
if you made a grave mistake with letting me go— baby, you
made a grave mistake when you told me we would build lemon
trees out in the back / we would climb mountains across the country bluff /
we would build a house filled with ceiling high glass windows and a kitchen
with cabinets and wood we picked out on the same day you told me
never to worry about you, about us. if there's nothing you hold sacred,
how do you sleep at night? you only fall asleep when i wake
to watch the sunrise, i know this. you used to call when you wanted
to sleep earlier, i know this. baby, you made a grave mistake letting me go,
but if it's truly sacred then maybe it wasn't meant for you in the first place.

—and if i'm trying to tell the truth, it's all bad

let the rain fall into your eyelids; use your well kept nails to pry open your eyes;
the eyes that promised me to never lie / you're an honest man, i know —
i know, but you lied the day we met / you lied the moment you said
you keep your promises / i know, but i let myself believe it anyways

let the rain fall into your eyelids; let the water burn and sink deep into the nerves
that have twisted themselves so tightly around your sense of reality;
you don't even know who you are. do you look in the mirror and ask where you went
wrong — "she's gone, she's gone, she's *gone*."

i remember i used to tell you how i wished you would feel / i wanted your heart to hurt.
i wanted it to burn in pain and make you feel like your thoughts were on fire.
you're an honest man, you know / you loved me wrong at the end, you know /
you know so you told me, again and again and again.

let the rain fall into your eyelids; being blind in pain for a moment
will make you see how i've gotten used to standing under thunderstorms and
induce endorphins when i feel the thunder reverberating inside of me /
i imagine what it would feel like if lightning struck me —

you're an honest man, i know — you would tell me i'm being stupid.
i think i hate honest men now; i want someone who lies to me;
i want to let lightning strike twice — i want my eyelids to burn
and i want someone who will burn with me until we're blind.

—i smile so wide when i hear lies; i smile so wide when it rains

i braid my hair, and i pull at the end—
maybe that'll help my hair grow longer.
i so badly want to be a different person
than who i was with you— i stand on my tip toes;
maybe that'll help me see clearer. sometimes
i shower three times a day and really scrub my skin.
remnants of memories don't wash well, and i know that now—
so bars of soap melt away quicker. i count on my fingers
under the hot water, how many bars of soap have i used
in the last four months? i braid my soaking wet hair,
and i pull at the end. i let it dry that way; letting the water
soak into my scalp— the fleeting worry of sickness
appearing until it gets buried with another worry—
another memory— i want to forget, so i make myself forget;
i so badly want to be a different person— so i scrub
hard until my head feels heavy; three times yesterday
and maybe four times today— it won't hurt to open up
the last bar of lavender soap that's been waiting in the back
of my cabinet; i smell the wrapper like you used to do
before throwing it away— that used to make me fall more in love with you.
now it just smells like lavender. nothing more;
i so badly want to be a different person than who i was with you—
so i stand on my tip toes; maybe that'll help me see clearer.

—pain sticks harder on skin than soap can wash off

when we analyze pleasure, do we destroy the beauty of it?
how fragile it must be— i like being captured by lenses
that refract light— my reflection
has always been foreign to me; in a sense, i have no idea
who i am. how fragile— to destroy beauty
with each passing thought; in a sense, destruction breeds
constant questions. i like being captured by lenses
to understand why i like to analyze pleasure for others
to question who they are. how fragile i must be—
pleasure is a fleeting thought that breeds destruction.
who i am in refracted light, reflected in mirrors
that shine against the sun— analyzing how
the brightness around me does not brighten the dullness
in my eyes. how fragile pleasure must be—
i have to ask questions in order to understand who i am.
in a sense, the destruction of beauty is almost necessary.
pleasure is a fleeting moment— lenses capture it if not
for a moment, these fleeting moments—
the fragility of it all brightens
my eyes and i'm starting to understand. i like
analyzing— until i've crumbled pleasure into fleeting
moments of beauty— until they're gone.

—things change, change with it

only my eyes can see the outlines of the plants in my room,
highlighted by a hue of red and then green and then blue
and the lights change every night, but the tears that threaten my eyes
stay the same. they stay at the brim, uninvited but cozied in as if at home—
only my eyes can see what you've been doing for yourself.
you stay silent most times, but when you talk
i am reminded of the fallacies of my heart.

i feel so selfish, you know, for wanting you to grow
with me. but i am reminded, you can lead a horse to the water
but you cannot make him drink it.
i am reminded of the late nights and early mornings
we would stay up talking about our dreams.
i used to drink more water than you, i think.
i am reminded of the fallacies of my heart—
emotion over reflection;
how could i ever be angry with you? oh, but i am
so angry. i feel selfish, you know, i want you to

swim *with* me. only my eyes can see
how the lights change every night like cars that stop
and then go and then slow down; *slow down,*
i tell my tears. i am reminded of the night i called you
as i cried— i know i used to drink more water than you.
the outlines of the plants in my room almost glow
and i am so proud of them.
reflection over emotion, i tell my thoughts.
drink until you're satisfied, i tell the horse.
i miss the nights we would stay up talking about our dreams,
how could i ever be angry with you? you're finally drinking the water.

—only my eyes see how you grow so well without me

Varsha Iyer

i've had the same nightmare the last two nights. i wake at 2:30AM,
looking at my palms shaking. in my dreams, i drown a little girl in a lake
i used to visit during summers as a child. when her face floats back up,
her features resemble mine— she could be me but i never stare at her
for longer than i need to. it doesn't matter anyway. this morning,
i woke up and i ordered an $80 bottle of CBD oil. maybe, this will help me
sleep at night without drowning faces that look like mine. i stare at myself
in the mirror sometimes and i remind myself i should give myself more grace.
i deserve more than this pain. i know this. so, i know.

the last two nights, i wake at 2:30AM. this is a confession:
i think about you sending songs to your new girlfriend that i have shown you
and i throw up. i used to pride myself in eating fruit every night
but when the vomit is bright red from the cherries i ate the night before,
i think i'd rather stick to eating nothing at all. my gut is so connected
to my heart— but it doesn't matter anyway. this morning, i woke up
and i ordered an $80 bottle of CBD oil. maybe, this will help me

erase each memory that has sunk deeply into my gut tying knots
until my breathe is constricted. the less i know the better, but i know
too much already. everytime i close my eyes, i see the little girl
i drown. it makes me sad. i want to help her, so i reach my arm out
but only after i have drowned her. i am so stupid sometimes. peace can come
after death, but never in the way i hope so i bury my hope for now,
until i can dig it back up later and find it again. i stare at myself in the mirror
after i vomit sometimes and i remind myself i should give myself
more grace. i deserve more than this pain. i know this. so, i know.

—maybe the CBD oil will help me sleep

65

candles can't tell time— it makes me sad.
their existence weighs on our fingers kissing flames
for fun. it's almost worrisome how i still cannot
stomach listening to Sade. sometimes when i'm driving
down the freeway i attempt to, but my breath always
catches and time runs out and i forget where i am.
the burning sensation ties itself into knots
and my fingers turn black— i melt into who i was
and forget what i am. fingers kissing flames
should bring warmth; i miss the smell of lavender
and i miss the smell of vanilla and i miss the smell of you.
by your side, i stopped worrying about candles—
for just a moment, for just a moment—
i worried about you.
sometimes when i'm driving
i think about how candles can't tell time.

—it makes me sad

under these same trees, i lost myself loving you.
i often forget the moment trees are cut in half
in order to become a field of homes. i attempted again
and again— with the same fear leaves shake with,
i ache to be cut in half / i ache to be left like a tree
with only its beginnings ripped open.

never led on the right path to return home, i lost myself
loving you. under the same trees, i realize i repeat
steps of growth like an involuntary habit of being cut in half.
i feel taller, i feel / my roots / am i the same
tree i was before? i ache to be cut in half again;
the desire to be hurt can be addicting
when you know you'll be a field of homes.

i realize i repeat steps of growth in order to return home
to you— i was wrong to assume these failed attempts
will work / i feel taller but i am only rooted in ripped beginnings
and i ache to be cut in half. under these same trees,
i remember i am the same tree i was before but the colors
of my leaves change without shaking. i often forget the moment
i found my way to a field i've never been to. am i the same
tree i was before? i often forget / i ache / i feel

—under these same trees, i'm ripped open again

you told me the best pieces written
are always the most difficult to digest;
i want to make this one the hardest pill
for you to swallow— let it catch in your throat
and let it take four glasses of water to
wash it down. after feeling discomfort
at the conjuncture of where you used to say
how you believed in something
and where you now don't say a word,
let the pain grow. it's a slow burn, i know;
i felt it back in May— then in June— back then,
i didn't understand you can't keep ash
from fires that burn too quickly. you cannot keep
lovers apart and expect distance to disappear.

—it's a slow burn, i know; but i stung quick

Varsha Iyer

i forgive my mistakes for being so harsh to me.
its impending consequences ignite fear
yet i remain calm; high tide hasn't arrived yet.

waves continue to shift in intensity, and i forgive
but don't forget in order to record each intensity
as if there's a pattern for it all; yet there are no rules

but the ones we create for ourselves. my mistakes
are an extension of myself and i remind myself
to be more kinder, to be more accepting— to me.

     —high tide is seconds away. and i remain calm

ambiguity is for assholes, or so i say. then i look in the mirror
and i wail. i've never liked being vague— it's— *shh*!
when i write, the more specific i am, the deeper i dive.
or so i say, but when the truth is said— i've never wanted to
be face to face with ambiguity so bad. honesty is sometimes worse,
or so i say, then i look in the mirror and remember i am made
for better things. or say they say, who am i to be made for things
that do not know me yet? they do not know i play symphonies
in my head when the lights are off; i weep, until the truth is said—
when i write, i've never been one for ambiguity. or so i say,
when i am face to face with the version of me submerged under fog.
i cannot see. and i'm incapable of breathing— yet, it's a choice;
i don't want to come up for air, if i am— *i am*; maybe if i am
honest, maybe i should like being an asshole for a change.

—arrogance is the symphony of the ignorant

the last time you and i went to get ramen you asked the waiter
for lemons for my water; it was the first time because— i usually order
for us because you cannot control your laughter when i ask for
a fork. after our first ramen date, you bought me metal chopsticks
and told me to learn: "you have to. next time, surprise me."

i keep them tucked beneath our design journal, your love letter
when we couldn't see each other for months before you said
fuck it— "i miss how you kiss me while you hold my arm when i drive."
i buried them under books i have never read— i do not plan to.

with lemons in my water, you looked at me inquisitively before asking:
"does your mom hate me because i broke your heart?"
i wanted to say: "no, but i do." instead, i laughed—
and asked the waiter for a fork because you didn't.

— "i thought you learned with the chopsticks?" "no."

i drove past your house just to see if i still remembered the way
there are routines we created and now i do them alone
there's a fear that hasn't yet escaped me or maybe
it's waiting for me to escape first

i think of the moment i'll see you again
i think i'll vomit before i want to hug you again
i'll want to hear about how much you've learned about yourself
and i'll want to hear things i already know rather than what i don't
so i can cry about it later, again

your family took apart the trampoline in the backyard;
i held my breath passing your driveway
to see it empty, what a *relief!*

i played the smiths and watched my pretty face turn red and tired
in the rearview mirror before i turned into a parking lot off of your street
and i exhaled everything i was holding in
i've gotten good at holding my breath for longer than i need to

i've gotten pretty good at accepting that you're gone because i asked you to go
until days like these when i know you'd walk out to my car if i asked you to
and you'd tell me that it'll be okay but i'd vomit before you even opened your mouth

you would say that it is fascinating i am still like this
i dig for depth and you dig for curiosity
my pockets are filled with receipts for gas and a tube of chapstick we used to share
i think of the moment i'll see you again
i'll want to tell you how much i've learned about myself
and tell you i've finally finished this damn book even though it's been so hard

you would tell me how proud of me you are
but i'd vomit before you could even get the words out

—i listened to pretty girls make graves by the smiths
on repeat and think about how you could've written this song

Varsha Iyer

i freeze time to my liking / it's a habit i'm trying to quit
i've been facing my fears head on / since you,
my capacity has only grown / to my liking,
nothing follows a certain set of rules anymore /
i design fate— and i design my actions /
my voice has become so loud / i'm not quite used to it yet
so i record myself just to play it back /
it's a habit i'm trying to make stick / to my liking,
new routines are getting easier to learn /
my capacity won't reach an end / i design fate / since you,
i face every fear i have until they're behind me.

    —the process of becoming whole again

how can i look up at the sky and not think of you
the stars are so much brighter when you're on a mountain—
it makes sense; you think of yourself because you can
and i— can only really think of you. i see Venus
to my right and you to my left, but you're not really there.
when you're on a mountain and it's just you—
are the stars brighter? if a tree falls down in a forest
and no one is around to hear it, does it still make a sound?
how can i look up at the sky and not understand why
you want to be in space, alone? now, it makes sense;
you'll see Venus to your right but all that's left
is just you. the stars are so much brighter

—and i almost cried looking at the sky tonight

Varsha Iyer

how honest are you being with yourself
and how much of that honesty is unbiased?

—letting you go is one of the hardest things i've ever had to do

often, i catch glimpses of myself. in different pictures
taken from different cameras. i do not look the same / i look
in the mirror, and then down at my hands, small
to me, to others capable of so much— i find myself
in specific features of myself that i can't stop staring at.
my lips purse as if they want to say something, and yet
i don't and i tilt my head to focus on my nose and then my eyes.
uneven, asymmetrical— often, i feel my heart pounding
louder than my voice and i know i need to ground myself, and yet
i cannot remember what i look like. which version
am i? i am most like what i see when i close my eyes and think
of myself. capable of so much, my voice yearning, i look like— i am

—trying to make something of myself

Varsha Iyer

the leaves that shake in the sun have only just begun. they've just been born, unfurling
at the sight of the sun peaking through suburban homes and concrete high rises.
the new warmth that has felt so far away for so long has come close, and i—
back to myself.
the leaves that shake don't stop growing; they dance among the breeze watching, waiting
for birds to come find a home alongside themselves. they move so freely,
and i often wonder if the leaves that shake, shake because they're desolate.
do they shake to seduce the birds?

they shake at a pace unbeknownst to themselves; leaves unfurling furiously,
each movement beckoning a new tune from birds whose wings have grown tired
from flying south to north after days where wind dominated their desires.
company is kept when those who keep it, keep it with no agenda. freely—
i often wonder how it would feel to find a home among the leaves that dance,
watching as if i had been waiting for myself to return all along— unfurling slow at first,
and then quicker until i've nestled deep into the dance,
swaying to silent tunes that never end.

—like seasons that change, i come back to myself

does ability matter without the attempt and action behind it?
you say you're better now— yet you still sleep more hours than you're awake.
you say you're better now— but the last time you were alone with your thoughts,
you stared at a wall for three hours and felt an irrational amount of anger.
what are you angry about?
does ability matter without the attempt and action behind it?
do you feel sorry for yourself in order to create a false sense of empathy?
does it makes you feel better about being irrationally angry?
the bad days happen so the good days will follow.
you say you're better now— do you journal every night?
you say you're better now— do you constantly ask yourself questions in order to reflect?
does continuous self-examination always mean progression in one's sense of self?
aren't you tired of knowing you have the ability to be better?
what's the difference in "i'm better," and "i'm being better,"?
does it matter?
the bad days happen so the good days will follow.

—6 mo. post-therapy, circa April 27, 2020

ah, to know myself— again, i haven't had the pleasure.
oh Miss, it's raining outside. do you enjoy it still?
to see others, and to understand they will understand me again.
i am not alone. you see, oh Miss, when i look in the mirror—
again, i haven't had the pleasure of meeting myself.
to know myself— long ago, it is not the same. here i stand,
not as soft or as naive. here i stand, i am tired— let me sit.

oh Miss, it's your favorite song. do you enjoy it still?
to see others, and to understand some will go but others will stay
unexpectedly; you will never understand. but i must know
i am not alone. you see, some will leave but more often,
there will be those who come to show you how the rain falls
upon the sidewalk at such an angle; do you enjoy it still?
the pleasantries are whisked away with the wind, ah—
the hello's and the goodbye's are buried under birch trees. you see,
oh Miss, to know myself— again, i haven't had the pleasure.

—looking in the mirror, seeing someone else each time

i dream of dipping my fingers into a koi pond. letting each fish graze my skin,
softly until their hues of white and orange are so bright it's the only thing i can see.
i want to watch them swim in circles, following each other from behind—
i wonder, if it is done blindly or if they choose who follows and who leads; and why, *why*

can i hear the sounds of the city nestled in suburbia? isn't that strange—
i can hear it so loudly;
the smell of sage overwhelms my thoughts and i lay upside down,
dreaming of how honey is so sweet. translucent gold dripping slowly
while sticking at the same time—i wonder, if it made a deal with gravity
to not be held captive at the same speed as the rest of the world.

my thoughts rarely arrange themselves in order. first comes, my future.
then comes, *you*. and after, white, satin curtains that fly in the breeze from open windows
while the sun seeps into my skin. isn't that strange—
i dream of much more while already being submerged into much more—
i can hear it the city so loudly; i can feel each fish grazing my skin;
i can taste the honey on my tongue

—and, i can't help but want more

i have always been so organized. when i was little,
i would ask my mom if i could sit in shopping carts
as she grocery shopped. i would rearrange every item
she bought like it was a game of Tetris. i fell in love
with the way shapes would fit so geometrically aligned
with one another; like things that were once a puzzle
are now whole, and i made it happen. me, myself, i—

i felt autonomous over organization. maybe
that's why i loved it so much— to make things whole
under my jurisdiction, in my own kingdom. i was happy
me, myself, i— knowing i was in control and that the consequences
of my decisions never ended in heartbreak. i learned
to trust this way— there is always a cause for an effect, and
if you played the game right, you'd never reach the end.

—strategy is key, organization is the lock

i feel like i'm 14 again, talking to you.
chewing on pink bubble gum, blowing big bubbles,
blushing wildly, hair messily dyed in streaks from blue Kool-aid,
i giggle at my phone with the screen so bright
late at night under the covers. i feel like i'm 14 again,
and it's easy to locate where on my body i'm feeling from.
the air seems less thick of skepticism, and i find pleasure
in believing everything i can. daydreaming of being close,
flipping through magazines that have no useful information,
i soak in colors that remind me of you— i feel so much
and i blame the butterflies in my stomach; i'm scared of them,
and i feel like i'm 14 again. i want you to catch them for me—
trap them in the palm of your hands and swallow them
as my lips touch yours— as i'm blushing wildly, talking to you.

—it's that middle school forever type love with you

Varsha Iyer

i have this bad habit i can't seem to kick—
i get an itch to skip the sad parts of TV shows
i rewatch for the hundredth time; it's only natural.

you do this thing when i say something that isn't true—
your eyebrows raise and your pretty brown eyes dilate
and you instinctively pull me closer to you; god, it is so
pure and i feel so safe when you tell me what is true.

i have this bad habit i can't seem to kick—
if you never take the risk, how do you expect to win?
so i take risks and i watch them unravel; it's only natural.

you do this thing when i kiss your cheek—
your pretty brown eyes close and your nose scrunches up
and you instinctively smile though you try to hide it; god
it is so pure and it makes me so happy to know you feel it too.

—it's only natural

i can't get you out of my head; trust me, i've tried.
i've never been the best at accepting things for what they are—
not everything has to feel like something else;
not everything has to be dug up from under soil to find its roots.
but leaves still stay green, and vines wrap around my body
until they've made a home in my head. these thoughts
have no roots but they've grown so tall so quickly;
i've never been the best at knowing how to enjoy the moment
before it's too late— trust me, i can't get you out of my head.
i've tried but you remind me as i return to you; it's as simple
as that— we know what we know and we don't what we don't.
leaves still stay green, vines wrap around my body
until you've made a home in my head.

—you make trees grow inside my head

Varsha Iyer

"i want to protect you," something that has always
been only said from a distance— never up close,

i've always been sunken deep in the land of supply and demand
i supply more than i demand; my eyes meet yours to tell you
a story— between left and right i forgot there were two more
ways of knowing how to love; up and down; it's a spiral
either way— protect me, see, i captivate you with my gaze
for a reason, see, it's only to show you what i mean, see.

up close, things seem out of focus— you have to really try
and it's never easy the first time until you make it easy yourself.
from a distance, i see but i want to come up close, anyways.
it's a tricky mind game— see, up and down mean more
than left and right anyways so what's the difference if we move
on a different timeline than the rest? it's ours, anyways, right?

i know the heat from each day drains you out, and i know
how your heart overwhelms you a lot and i know you want to know
how the same thoughts run in mine— are they as fast as yours?
do they skip out of order? do they hurry? baby, baby, *baby*—

sit back and relax; overanalysis is paralysis— there's a reason
we don't play mind games with each other, see, there's a reason
we cut to the chase and found ourselves at the center of the sun, see
you must fall to fall in love but we've both been flying up, see.

"i want to protect you," something that has always
been only said from a distance— never up close,

                    —how high can we fly up, how far can we go?

85

let's play Twister— two hands on green, and one leg on red
        self control really is a mind game for you and i—
        and so our legs never touch the red; it's that easy

when you tilt your head to the side and tell me everything that's on your mind,
i want to take my hand off green and place it against your cheek— so soft
and listen to everything you have to say until you run out, and then maybe

let's play Twister— you're helping me meet myself for the first time,
        and i realize it's not funny at all at how i want to make you laugh all the time,
        and get twisted in everything but mind games; we can make it that easy

maybe, one leg on red is better than two; self control really— is just about ourselves;
you get twisted in my thoughts as easily as i get nervous thinking about you
and sometimes, i want to take my hand off green and place it against your cheek;

—i like who i am with you, so let's play Twister

Varsha Iyer

the way your hand fits behind my head, holding me up
i could lay there forever, under you;
i could hear you say my name, it's one of my favorite words to hear
from your lips other than when you talk about what you love to do—
your eyes almost glisten / and you find yourself again, i see it;

the way you pull me close to kiss my forehead—
feeling your heartbeat get faster,
i could make you laugh until your stomach hurts
and make you admit things with a sheepish smile when you're wine drunk
just to make your heart do *that* thing until mine does the same;

you are something else— has anyone told you that recently?
you are; your voice— is turning into my favorite song; i could hear you
talk for hours about everything that's going on in your head—
the way your lips touch mine— i could lay there forever,
under you; hold me up—and say my name; don't dream of something else, baby

                    —*just dream of me*

i won't overthink if you don't overthink;
20% royalties off of this book— 50% of my thoughts
and 30% of your lips on mine. trapping lightning bugs
in my throat and i like watching you watch them light up
when you tell me you've been thinking about me.

each eyelash we make wishes on sends
another lightning bug free when i blow them away.

i won't overthink if you don't overthink; but
maybe i am in over my head— i can't stop thinking
about the first audio message you ever sent me.
30% of my poetry— 50% of my thoughts
and 20% royalties off of this book.

each eyelash we make wishes on sends
another reason to kiss you over and over, my way.

—now you know what i wished for, huh?

those seconds in between knowing what i feel and knowing what you feel—
i have to catch my breath; i remember you said it first but
now i feel it more. those seconds in between
make me forget my name, *wait*, who am i, again, to you, who am i—
i've always liked to hear you say it out loud. i like when you give substance to what
once did not exist. i've always liked it when you add my name at the end.
those seconds in between what i feel for you and knowing what you feel for me—
i have to stop myself from smiling too wide. i know i'll make you say it again,
wait, remind me of my name, who am i, to you, who am i—

—yours

ask her what she wants,
she'll say
something sweet—

she'll say
she'll hold you down, through whatever
she'll hold you,
down

ask her what she wants,
she'll say to watch you unravel
she wants something sweet,
and watching you unravel is the sweetest
thing she has come across.

tell her something sweet,
unravel into the palm of her hands
and ask her and she'll tell you

what you're made up of.

                    —something sweet, so sweet

Varsha Iyer

we cherry pick under a red sun— dark,
        thick, heavy fogs spread above us but we inhale. it can't be good
        for us, but it's good enough. the cherries are so bitter,
we have to wait for a little more, but my teeth tingle at the sight of cherries
and my lips ache to be stained by every shade of red cherries paint.
        under a red sun— i know you know
but i'll tell you a hundred more times— we can talk all we want
but cherries are meant to be picked and we're meant to eat them
until we are so full our eyes glaze over and we cannot stop smiling.

we cherry pick under a red sun— hazy,
        i know you know but i'll tell you a hundred more times—
        i am there on the good and the bad days
we have to wait a little more, but my tongue searches for cherry seeds in your mouth
and my fingertips want to touch the back of your neck and apply enough pressure
        to make you hold me closer— under a red sun,
the cherries are so bitter so we'll cry every once in a while in hopes
they'll turn sweet without waiting, without eyes glazing but you know i know
it isn't easy that but i hope anyways— like a fool drunk off cherries

—we can talk all we want but cherries are meant to be picked

91

these waking moments we spend together
we lean back on passenger seats
it's like we're drunk on being friends
so we kiss on each other a little extra
and blame it on the wine
and maybe if it's the wine's fault
this is justified
so let's play old Justin Timberlake
and laugh until we forget the time
we can pretend we're not as messy as we really are
and maybe if it's the wine's fault
we can kiss on each other a little extra
there's something about these moments
i think that you know
i can only smell cotton candy
and taste sugar on your lips
i want to celebrate you
and call you baby in your ear
to make your fingers grip my waist a little tighter
turn Futuresex / LoveSounds up, *baby*
i think that you know
we can pretend we're not as messy as we really are
and it's only you and me for right now
minus all the other shit
so we lean back on passenger seats
until the album is over
and time is up
and we realize this is only really fun
until it's not

                    —*got me LoveStoned*

Varsha Iyer

i lost the feeling of fall. it whisked away, so surely—
and i still remember looking at you through my rearview mirror.
when i drive, i have the windows down, and i always look up
and wish i had a sunroof. the wind whisks away yellow and red leaves, so surely—

strands of my hair tangle within and without, and i remember
smiling so wide after leaving your house. for a split second,
i had remembered what hope felt like. i hadn't felt it in months
and i felt it each time i saw you. but it whisked away, so surely—

as did the breeze that shook the trees outside my room window
and as did each day i spent in bed wondering if time was playing tricks
on me as if it was April. my best friend reminds me—
"hope is only half the fight; you will spend hours detangling your hair."

the way you danced back home so happily will always taste sweet on my tongue,
like how i imagine hope would taste. so i dance around my room the days we don't speak
and watch the trees outside dance with me. i know everything will be whisked away,
so surely, and i'm feeling a little cold but at least for now— i have hope.

—one day, time will be on my side. until then, i have hope

is accommodation the same thing as adaptation—
or am i growing in the wrong direction? see, i think i
have accommodated myself to the circumstances
i have been given but i have not yet adapted
to my surroundings. i do not cry as often, but
i keep to myself / it's the only way things make sense
anymore. secrets that are secrets equals silence
you can trust. i do not cry as often, but
that makes me worry. am i adapting
to a new way of coping or am i growing
in the wrong direction? i keep to myself /
i try not to think about what i have lost. why
focus on walking backwards if i can focus
on walking with my eyes closed? see, i think i
have accommodated myself to the circumstances
i have been given but i have not yet adapted
to my surroundings. i have my eyes closed, anyways
so all directions will lead me astray.

—step by step, adapting to what i cannot see

Varsha Iyer

fear can be a good thing;
indulge in what you can.
because when it's gone, it's gone.
we fear so we neglect;
but we cannot neglect what is true.
there are multiple tracks of truth—
each with its own feeling, its own details
why don't we let truths co-exist freely anymore?
we find ways to let the tracks exist just to destroy
the one that is harder to hear.
why don't we ever want to do the work anymore?
and they ask so kindly not to be ignored.
so please, baby let's not ignore them together—

—why don't we let truths co-exist freely anymore?

i hang upside down from my bed to realize the wicked truth. the truth is
my heartbeat has been living in my throat for the past three days
and i know exactly why: i am waiting for something that will never happen.
we deem imperfection as something to strive for because we cannot be perfect,
and i still try— until all of my thoughts have fallen out of my head because
i have been hanging for hours. the blood is rushing to my brain
and it's the first time in days i am focused on something other than my heartbeat.
what was yesterday is not what is now, and i have to build from the ground up
after i have destroyed and eaten the remains from yesterday. the wicked truth
is change is inexorable and routines have to be restructured when you feel
your heartbeat in your throat again. in three days, it will be gone—

—following your dreams mean things won't work until they do

Varsha Iyer

my name is being said in rooms i haven't walked into yet;
how funny— the ideas you've been talking about, baby
i turned them into real things. i walk into my dreams
and i sit pretty on top of words i've been thinking about
for far too long. everything i've ever wanted is already
in my hands; how funny— look at how fucking intricate these ideas
have gotten and how beautiful they look when they're made
into real things. i walk into my dreams and i walk out
with new ones; so keep talking, baby i'll be busy
making the things you talk about real.

—when one door opens, i walk in

why do i die so much in my own dreams?

it's a slow process; slicing every inch of fear
to find the excitement at the root of it.

the things that travel from my subconcious to my concious
travel with ease; i see progress— i am thankful.

things don't look the same in real life, but
i have accepted death for what it is. i feel free;

application matters more than just realizations
so i keep working; it all comes down to a choice: to choose yourself or not

i die every night in my own dreams,
a different story forces the pressure to bleed.

if the next thing is the next thing, you must finish
what is before, before the next. i feel free;

i accept to adapt; don't you?
a different story is next but before, before the next i am here.

it all comes down to a choice: to choose yourself or not
so i keep working; i feel free.

—letting it hurt before i can heal

Varsha Iyer

how dangerous it is to think
"i will miss this when it's over,"
in the present moment

—let the present hold you

i often think about how the future feels on my skin
the truth is it's intimacy that's the *bitch*!

have you ever wanted to give someone your whole world
because you knew they deserve it more than you do

to adore someone wholeheartedly is to enjoy the silence
in its purest form, but first you must learn how to be still

i think i'd really rather be a form of fruition than a form of erosion

let me lay deep under soil, nails gritted in grime
and let blades of grass sever through my flesh and grow tall
let the seeds carve out crevices and let roots bury me deep
wrapped around until i cannot see and cannot hear

i'd rather be a form of fruition than
someone who digs in the dirt to find places you got hurt

i'm trying to enjoy the silence, i am but
it's intimacy that's the *bitch*!
i often think about how the future feels on my skin

it rained yesterday so the soil is soft
and today, i can feel myself start to change

                    —the day you plant the seed is not the day you eat the fruit

Varsha Iyer

notice the patterns,
acknowledge the repetitive actions and intentions,
understand what works and what doesn't—

unlearn, relearn, and move forward.

progression is messy, but
slow waves are waves still made
regardless of low or high tide

                    —the cycle never ends

Made in the USA
Columbia, SC
27 December 2020